AM: To my late sister Yvonne
And my husband Carl who
rescued Minnie Minor

JB: For Sam and Alice

Minnie Minor
My Tropical Island Dog

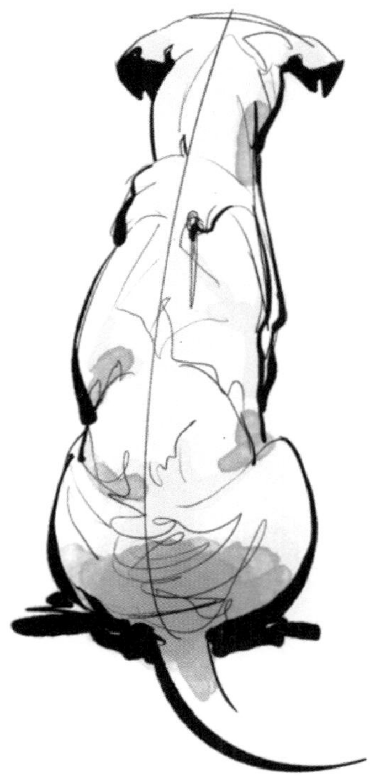

Adele Maxwell-Miles

Illustrated by Jake Biggin

I am alone, I have no home,
no food or water to drink,
The sun's so hot
it's burnt my skin
and made my ears go pink,

I walk the beach to find something to eat
and grab a washed-up fish.

It's not enough to fill me up,
a hearty meal is what I wish.

The day is hot, the beach is full,
I don't know where to go,

So there I dig,
and dig a hole,
and lie down very low,

But some kind lady sees my
plight and beckons me to come,

A bowl of water just for me, I
think she is my mum.

This kind lady I call my mum,
she gives me food as well,
I think she likes me quite a lot,
as far as I can tell,

No-one in my life has been as nice as she is to me,
I won't be told to go away, as far as I can see.

She has a man, I call him dad,
he's really very kind,
I follow them around the place,
they both don't seem to mind,
But one sad day mum goes away,
in a taxi with her case,
I run and run, it's very hard,
I don't give up the chase.

But now she's gone, I don't know why, or also what to do,
But dad's still here, I'm really pleased,
because I love him too.

My dad, he says, I'll take you home to
London Town- where's that?
I'll wait for him, he is so kind, and sit upon the mat,
Minnie Minor- it will be my name,
I think that's very grand,
But where he lives in London, there'll be no sea of sand.

Suddenly I'm in a cage, I really don't know why,
No more running on the beach, I say with a great sigh,
Fourteen hours I think they said, in a plane up in the sk
Then I'll be with mum and dad, so in this cage I lie.

The plane has landed -where am I- it's very cold outside.
My mum and dad are here at last,
they take me for a ride,

No sea or sand for me to run,
but buildings all around,
It's very strange, I'm scared of course,
with all the funny sounds.

My mum and dad live in a house,
its very nice and neat,
I've found a home at last I say,
and even got a seat,

But something's very strange,
I really do not know,
Some days I'm feeling very good,
and some days I feel low.

I think I'm going to be a mum,
oh dear,
oh dear,
oh dear.
How am I really going to cope,
with puppies to feed and rear?

They will be fun, I'm sure of that,
they'll eat and sleep and play,
That will keep me very busy,
all the night and day.

Now I have my children,
puppies one, two, three and four,
I really like them quite a lot,
but glad there are no more,
The puppies now are eight weeks old,
they go to homes afar,
That leaves me now to have a rest,
hurrah,
hurrah,
hurrah.

And now I have a mum and dad,
so happy do I feel,
Not alone, I have a home,
lots of kindness
and a meal,
I really am a happy dog,
as happy as can be,
Living now in London Town,
far away from beach and sea.

The End

Minnie's journey

Minnie Minor from Mauritius- the True Story

Over the years my husband Carl who worked for the Commonwealth and I have been fortunate to visit many countries. In 1997 Carl was at a conference on the beautiful African island of Mauritius in the Indian Ocean and I was able to go with him. However, I was very sad as my dear sister, Yvonne, had just died of cancer aged only 60.

In Mauritius we stayed at a beautiful seaside resort. While Carl was at his meetings, I befriended a scraggy little stray female dog on the beach. It was a hot day, and she was trying to hide under people's sun lounges to get into the shade but was shooed away by everyone. I felt sorry for her, so I brought her a bowl of water and let her sit with me. I then started to save my breakfast sausages and bacon for her each day which she devoured eagerly. She soon bonded with us and would follow us everywhere. We called her 'Minnie Minor' being much smaller than our English setter dogs at home.

On impulse, we decided to take Minnie to a local vet for anti-flea treatment but were horrified to be told strays were to be destroyed and then fed to the crocodiles. Thinking about Minnie being culled was very upsetting for us.

I left for home before Carl, and it was heart-breaking to see Minnie run and run after our departing taxi until she collapsed exhausted on the roadside. I had tears in my eyes. But when Carl returned to the hotel, she was loyally waiting for him in front of our beachside hotel room. When I arrived after my 14-hour flight home I received a text from Carl. It said Minnie is coming back with me to London! I was both amazed and delighted.

Getting Minnie back was no easy task as she had to get UK Ministry of Agriculture clearance and on arrival, she was forced to spend a miserable six months in quarantine, unnecessary as Mauritius is rabies free. Back she did come, flying on BA at some considerable expense, to say nothing of the subsequent quarantine fees.

Once in quarantine near London she was now locked up in a cold climate, having previously been free to roam at will on a warm beach. We visited her as much possible, but were very distraught that whenever we left again, she literally screamed for us to stay. Her love and affection for us was daunting and made us feel upset at having to leave her.

After a while, Minnie put on weight and the quality of her fur improved. However, we were in for a shock. One rescued dog turned into five when she unexpectedly bore four puppies. At this stage I thought we may have to re-mortgage our house to pay for all the new kennel fees. Absurdly the puppies, having been born in the UK, were released from quarantine after only a few weeks while poor little Minnie had to stay on without her pups.

This touching story hit the UK media with special features in the Sunday papers and Breakfast TV came to our garden to film the playful puppies. Soon we were deluged with requests to take in the sweet little dogs and were sent donations from across the country which we forwarded to the Mauritius dog charity MSPCA to help other strays.

All the puppies found a home and we were delighted when Minnie finally came out of quarantine after six long months in October 1997. She was to spend seven happy years with us and every day we could feel her deep love and gratitude for having rescued her, far away from her barren existence on a beach in Mauritius.
As result of our experience with Minnie I feel deeply for all the poor stray dogs wherever they may be. I hope that they will also find human kindness and love. I am therefore arranging for proceeds from the sales of this book to go to help other stray dogs get the support and affection which dear Minnie Minor received.

Adele Maxwell-Miles/Wright

Adele lives in London and Kent with her husband Carl Wright and their lively English setter Rupert. She had previously run Adele's Dance School for many years and her hobbies are writing poems, showing English setters, mosaicing sculptures and tropical gardening.

Printed by Amazon Italia Logistica S.r.l.
Torrazza Piemonte (TO), Italy

44415954R00016